THE BEGINNER'S GUIDE TO
Life Drawing

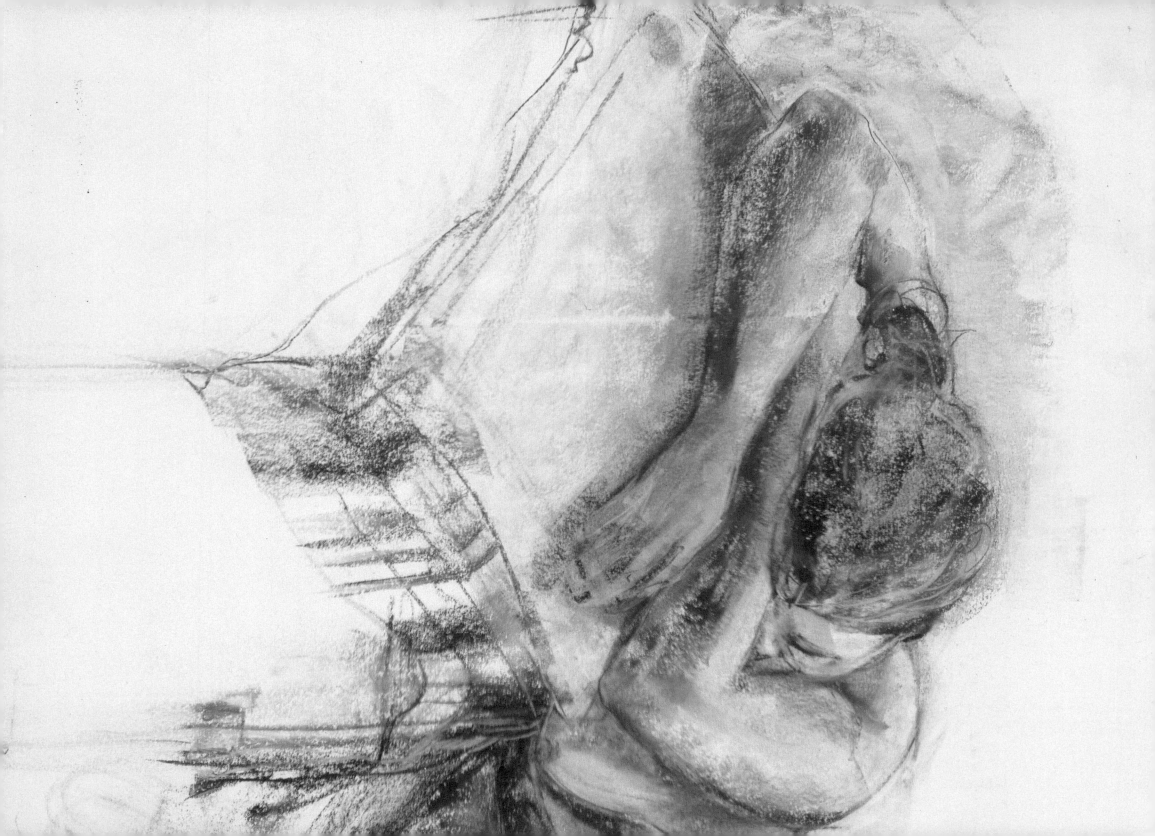

THE BEGINNER'S GUIDE TO
Life Drawing

Viv Levy

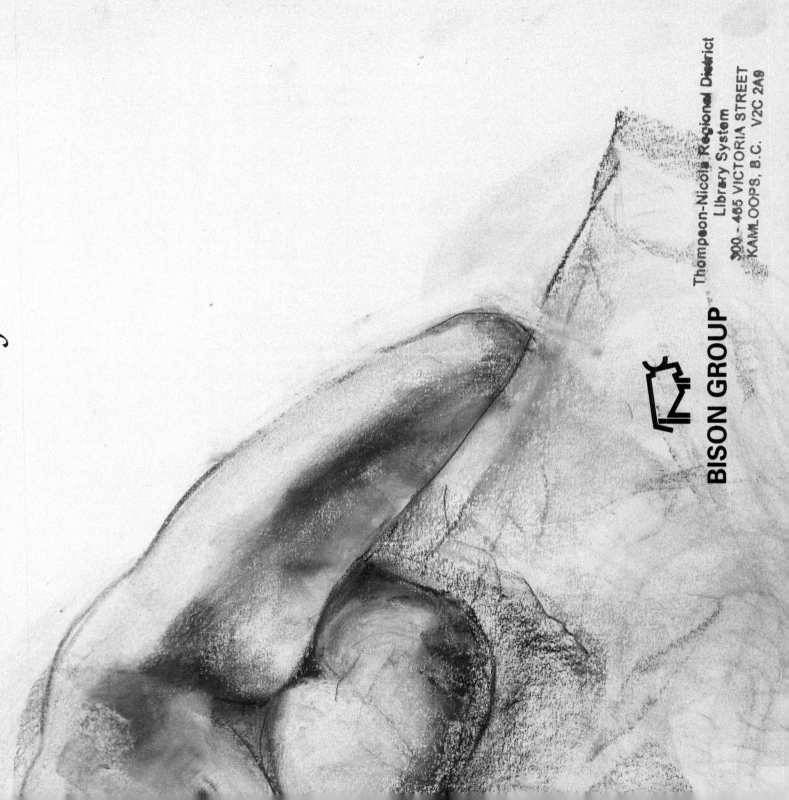

BISON GROUP

Thompson-Nicola Regional District
Library System
300 - 465 VICTORIA STREET
KAMLOOPS, B.C. V2C 2A9

First published in 1993 by
Bison Books Ltd
Kimbolton House
117A Fulham Road
London SW3 6RL

ISBN 0-86124-737-X

Printed in Hong Kong
Reprinted 1994

The right of Viv Levy to be identified
as the author has been asserted by
the same in accordance with the
Copyright, Designs and Patents Act 1988.

PAGE 1
Viv Levy: *Small Dog* Pencil
PAGE 2/3
Viv Levy: *Model with Cushion* Pastel
RIGHT
Dido Crosby: *Male Model on the Move* Pen and ink

Contents

Introduction

'The discipline of drawing endows the fantasy with an element of reality, thus lending it greater weight and driving power.'

This is a guide to a new language, a rich, universal language that speaks to the eyes. I am assuming that you have picked up this book with no preconceptions about how drawing should be taught. I will not be addling your brain with the mysteries of anatomy or the intricacies of the skeleton. Our anatomical structure is, of course, indispensable but this is a book about seeing and, unless you are blessed with X-ray vision, dealing with the parts you cannot see will only confuse you. My aim is to demystify, not to bombard you with the second-hand methodology of academe. Details of the internal anatomy become relevant once you have identified a particular problem, when perception belies understanding. I will not be encouraging you to dissect your victim and to name the parts, but to look at the subject in its entirety, to believe the evidence of your eyes, and to transfer what you have seen on to the page. Simple. Nothing must be taken for granted; you may assume that you know what a foot looks like but I'm willing to bet that you have never really LOOKED at one. Worthiness alone is not the key to learning and will do little to boost your morale; be prepared to enjoy yourself.

Before you transform that seductive, alarmingly pristine sheet of paper, before you make your first mark on it, and change it forever, then stick it on the wall or consign it to the bin, ask yourself why it is you want to draw. Have you always wanted to and is this, finally, it? Are you informing another passion, using drawing as the 'basis and theory of painting and sculpture' (Ghiberti), as the science of the arts? Have you come to improve your hand/eye co-ordination? Or will your drawings be entities in themselves? Silent poetry.

Drawing can be all or any one of these things, a service area or an end in itself. As stretching and limbering are to dance, practicing scales is to music, reading to writing, so drawing can instruct and enrich another discipline. But it is not just the basis and

theory. It does train hand/eye co-ordination, if you persevere; it can serve as an aide memoire, as raw material or as working plans for painting, sculpture or design. It is also, however, a language in itself, a language of mind minus words, a visual shorthand that will enable you to select, condense, distort, emphasize and re-invent your subject. It frees the subconscious, jogs the memory, forces you to look, teaches you to see. Whether you are limbering, recording or creating, it is essential that you believe the evidence of your eyes.

So why 'Figure' drawing? Is the unclothed

human figure the only form of life that qualifies for inclusion in this category? I imagine that few of us are blessed with an available nude, drifting around our homes, ready and willing to freeze into excruciating poses for us to draw, nor is it likely that we own huge mirrors, efficient heating and the privacy and confidence to disrobe and draw ourselves, warts and all. You may be consulting this book as a spur to get you to a formal Life Class, but it is more probable that you are looking for information and exercises to keep you going when other options are unavailable. My definition of 'Life', therefore, will include plants, animals and clothed figures; our familiars who are available, who will welcome all the attention and scrutiny we lavish on them and will not be unduly horrified, or insulted, by our first self-conscious attempts at their likenesses.

Why 'Life' when there's a world of inanimate objects just waiting to be drawn: architecture, museum collections, interiors, figments of the imagination, patterns and traces of memory? 'Life' is the ultimate challenge: a life drawing must seize the moment, convince the viewer that the sitting figure may rise, the sleeping dog may wake, the flowering plant may wither. The face reveals something about the mind; the stance,

human or animal, is a key to character; the condition of a plant is synonymous with the seasons changing.

In his *Testament Artistique*, Rodin said that 'Nature should be your Goddess'. Here is a lifetime's study; nature's astonishing mechanical inventions, juxtapositions of form, line and texture, constantly on the

LEFT
Viv Levy
Quince
8b pencil, 5½ × 4⅛ inches (142 × 105 cm) Portrait of my dog. I had to grab it in about thirty seconds; additional information was culled from years of looking and the experience of previous drawings.

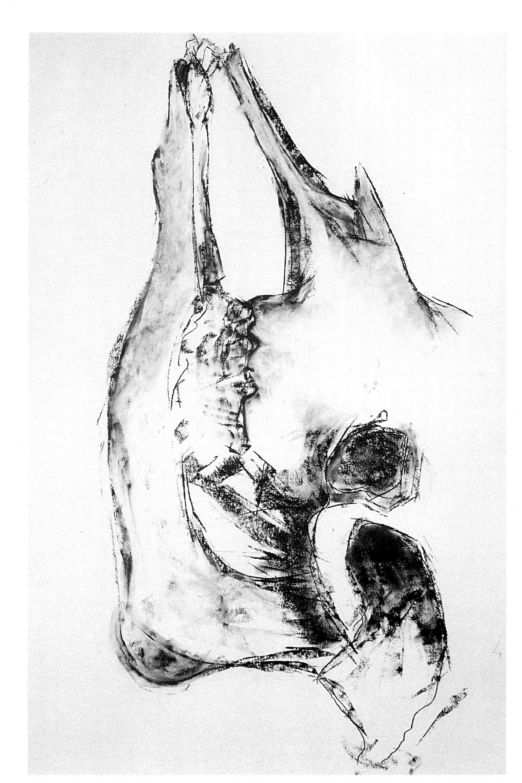

BELOW
Viv Levy
Giraffe Skull

INTRODUCTION

move, growing, changing color, surviving in the face of enormous odds. Imitate the way nature works, not the way she dresses, and you can't go wrong. Where better to look for the genesis of a drawing, a feast for the eye, a lesson. It is true that once you have really looked at a subject, once you have drawn it, you will never forget it.

Finally, ask yourself what constitutes a 'good' drawing. There is no pat answer. You will recognize it when you see it; it will bear the stamp of the individual who made it. This 'signature' has nothing to do with style, good taste or fashion; when drawings, or any work of art, are encumbered with self-conscious pre-occupations, truth flies out of the window. Empathize with nature, don't just record a pleasing corner of it; work with passion and concentration, energy and joy, and your unique character will emerge.

The drawing that comes from the serious hand can be unwieldy, uneducated, unstyled and still be great simply by the superextension of whatever conviction the artist's hand projects, and being so strong that it eclipses the standard qualities critically expected. The need, the drive to express can be so strong that the drawing makes its own reason for being. – David Smith, 1905-65, American sculptor.

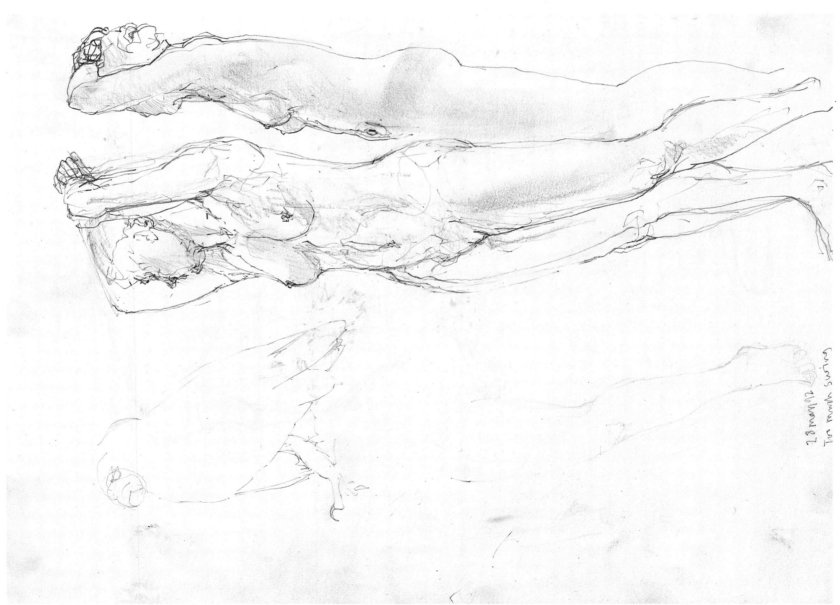

LEFT
Dido Crosby
Page from a sketch book:
Model on the Move
Pencil, 11½ × 8 inches (29.4 × 20.5 cm)
An elegant and spare drawing, but you nevertheless understand the back view and are able to imagine the model continuing slowly to move around, across and off the page. The faint drawing of the bird (top left) balances the composition and tickles the fantasy button.

1. How and Where to Start

Do not rush in, grab the first scrap of paper to hand, seize a magic marker, take a perfunctory glance at the subject and expect to dash off a stunning likeness. Choose your materials with care and set yourself up so that your concentration is not repeatedly broken by expeditions to the west wing for an eraser, another color or something more suitable to wear.

Choose and set up, or pose, your subject with care. Make sure that you have a good view. Animals are unpredictable so check that you are not adjacent to something for them to hide behind or under; you could find yourself spending the rest of the day talking to the underside of the sofa. Animals can also make excellent subjects, however. My dog is a natural performer and collapses into outrageous poses at the lift of a pencil, even in a crowded class.

Choose your paper with care. If you match the texture of the paper to the medium you are using you will already be ahead of the game (see Materials, page 16). Cut your paper to scale; do not worry about standard sizes, you may want to work in a circular format, in a square or on a long narrow strip (useful for moving figures). Do not start by making a giant drawing of a small plant, a life-sized drawing of a human figure or a miniature of an elephant; we'll talk about going against the grain later. Ensure that your paper is the right way up, i.e. 'landscape' or horizontal for reclining or horizontal poses, 'portrait' for standing or vertical. (Again there may be instances when you want to set your figures in opposition to the frame.)

Make sure that your paper is secured to a sympathetic surface. Judicious use of masking tape or bulldog clips before you start will spare you the torment of pursuing your work around the floor, chasing unpredictable marks around the page, creasing or tearing the page while erasing, or engaging in enthusiastic frottage.

Choose your medium with care. It must not only be capable of caressing the paper but should also flatter the subject. The delicate mark deposited by a soft HB pencil may

be the very thing for an intimate study of a dung beetle, but prove a useless ally for the sensual contours of a well-rounded female form or the fluid movements of a cat. The scale of the mark should be compatible with the size of the paper. Do not approach a 4 foot×6 foot expanse of paper brandishing an eyeliner brush, unless you fancy yourself as a budding pointillist, or confront a meager sketchbook with a dripping, six-inch house-

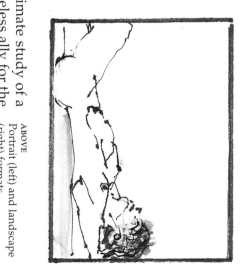

hold brush or a fistful of extra-soft charcoal (see Dictionary of Marks, page 19.)

Do not become addicted to one medium just because you feel secure with it. You are aiming to surprise yourself and enrich your vocabulary. Learn to enjoy losing control.

The way you arrange yourself, your stance, is as important as the comfort and well-being of your model. You may sit at a table, as long as only the hands and fingers need to travel across the page, but be sure that the table is not obscuring your view. You may squat on the floor for larger work, when the whole arm comes into play, or when you are using a wet medium and want to avoid drips. Remember that when you are working on a horizontal surface the thing that you are drawing will be perpendicular to you; you are not getting the same view of both the subject and the drawing. This dual perception causes images to become elongated on the page, especially with larger drawings. If you decide to prop your work on an easel or staple it to the wall, STAND UP and make sure that the center of the page is at, or just above, eye level. You will now be able to use your whole body. You will be able to continually stand back from the work, without causing an avalanche. Be sure there is nothing behind you; they say that sculpture is the stuff you trip over when you step back to admire a painting.

You need to be in the right frame of mind to pull off a lively drawing: a state of relaxed tension. You will need to be focused, brimming, quivering with concentration, with skinned eyes and a relaxed body. Don't clutch your pencil/pen/charcoal/brush, in a vice-like grip – it will not escape; and don't make infuriating little stabs at the paper. Be bold, be loose. Choose something interesting to draw. The world is your oyster, don't bore yourself into a state of indifference by picking an unsympathetic subject or a flabby pose. Be prepared to take chances and you will discover something new: when drawing takes over, amnesia sets in and time flies.

The American sculptor Alexander Calder (1898–1976) summed up the difficulties of drawing animals: 'The pose, or rather lack of pose, of the animal will often prove a disturbing element. Sometimes the beast will be reclining, probably asleep. Then unless

LEFT
Bryan Kneale
Moving Figure
Conté, 8⅛ × 11½ inches
(20.8 × 29.4 cm)
A relaxed arm and hand and focused looking result in a loose drawing that flows with the model.

ABOVE
The problem of drawing on a horizontal surface: the subject of the drawing and the work exist on different planes and you will undoubtedly get some distortion on the page (usually elongation of the image), which will become visible when you lift the work onto the vertical plane.

Viv Levy
Lady Weight Lifter
Same subject, different
media and focus:

LEFT
Oil pastel and turpentine
wash, 16¼ × 11¼ inches
(41.6 × 28.8 cm)
The model is placed low on
the page and the
background has been
cropped out.

BELOW
Charcoal and white pastel.
Here the model is placed
firmly on her plinth, further
up the page and with some
indication of the
background, which affects
the atmosphere of the
drawing.

he is in the throes of a nightmare, it will be easy sailing, provided you get a good vantage point. However, if he is on the move there may still be two possibilities. The animal may be repeating a cycle of motions, as a caged lion paces back and forth, or it may perform the action only once, as a dog may yawn. In the first case it is possible to wait and observe and study the action, thus building up one's knowledge with repeated views of the same thing. In the second instance, memory and impressionableness come into play very strongly as well as ease and speed of execution.

There is always a feeling of perpetual motion about animals, and to draw them successfully this must be born in mind. Remember that action in a drawing is not necessarily physical action. A cat asleep has intense action. When an animal is in rapid motion, keep rapidly transmitting your impressions of the animal's movement, and enjoy what you are drawing.

If you are drawing a human animal, don't worry if he/she breathes, twitches, droops, sneezes or scratches; incorporate the quirks and realities of being alive into your drawing. Don't blame the model for a bad drawing. Draw from photographs at your peril. Unless you have selected a particularly inept photograph, the camera will have done your editing for you. There is nothing left for you to do but to slavishly copy a view taken through a mechanical lens. Many people find it easier to work from two-dimensional images. It is as if being able to touch perspective makes foreshortening and illusion comprehensible; something or someone has digested your looking for you. Shutting one eye flattens three-dimensional objects. Be prepared to grimace, to measure, to peer at your work in a mirror, to look and to look and to look again until you understand what you see.

People and animals talk back. If you feel unnerved at the prospect of a conversation, other than the one you should be having with yourself and the drawing, start off by tackling a plant. Don't talk to that plant.

You have chosen your model; you have found the best view; you are poised, pen in hand. Wait – there is another decision to make. If this drawing is to be more than an adequate copy it must have a direction of its own, content and meaning, or it will be no more than the page of a diary which catalogues events without reference to atmosphere, feeling or humor.

Be ambitious.

2. Materials and Dictionary of Marks

Technique is what belongs to others.
Technique is what others call it when
you have become successful at it.
Technique as far as you are concerned
is the way others have done it.
Technique is nothing you can speak
about when you are doing it.
It is the expectancy of impostors.
    They do not show a
    respect for themselves
    or for what they are doing.

– David Smith

To an extent technique can be taught; it is a mechanical skill. Once you have mastered it, you can use it to serve inspiration and more or less forget about it. I have no secrets to disseminate; technique in drawing is so subjective that you may want to employ some means which is traditionally frowned upon to serve your needs. I will tell you some of the facts about materials and leave you to evolve your own technique. Only practice will improve manual dexterity. There are no magic formulae, so you should try things out for yourself, extend your range and don't trust other people's methods.

It is difficult to define the dividing line between drawing and painting. Some associate drawing with a dry medium and monochrome, painting with a wet medium and color, drawing with paper, painting with

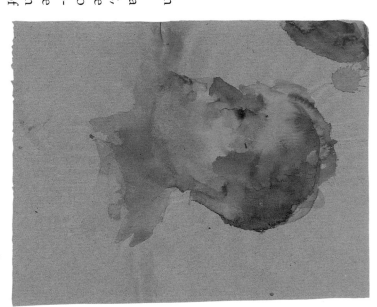

LEFT ABOVE AND BELOW
Viv Levy
Two drawings in watercolor, on brown paper.
Although the medium is wet, colored and applied with a brush, I consider these pieces to be drawings. The model was a colorful character but looked sad and tired that day; it was her 'look' that suggested the medium.

RIGHT
Leonardo da Vinci
A Star of Bethlehem and Other Plants, c.1505–08
Red chalk and pen and ink, 7¾ × 6 inches (19.8 × 16 cm)
No one would dispute the placing of this drawing in the 'study' category, but still it stands on its own as a great work, regardless of intention or function.

canvas. Pre-Renaissance drawing was made directly on to the wall and was then painted in. Leonardo da Vinci (1452-1519) changed this for ever by using drawing as a separate discipline, either as a plan on paper for a subsequent masterwork or as a study in itself. Do not allow any preconceptions you may have about the nature of drawing to restrict your ambition; experiment with materials and techniques.

Materials

I have already mentioned the importance of choosing paper and a medium appropriate to the task in hand. Obviously you will not want to spend a fortune at the outset. It is quite normal to lose all sense of proportion and go completely crazy in an art supplier's shop, ending up with an enormous collection of goodies that you will never use, and a large dent in your bank balance. Don't fall prey to expensive collections of pencils beautifully displayed in designer boxes. Breaking up the set will unhinge your mind.

The same goes for sketchbooks; exotically bound books of expensive hand-made paper will undoubtedly put the fear on you and inhibit your ability to let go. Don't buy ready-made kits. Someone has had a lot of fun putting temptation in your way but they cannot anticipate your needs.

My suggestions are:
1. A pile of very cheap paper, such as news-print, brown wrapping paper or old news-papers. You will have no compunction about ruining paper destined for the garbage; you may even improve it out of recognition. Some of my liveliest drawings

LEFT AND RIGHT ABOVE
Viv Levy
Moving Model
Stick and ink on the back of an envelope, stick and ink on newspaper.
Speed was of the essence here: scrap paper was all I could lay my hands on, the stick had parted company with a redundant sculpture, the ink was purloined, but I was able to knock out some drawings while simultaneously teaching a class. I enjoyed the unpredictable movement of the line and the random behavior of the ink on absorbent paper.

MATERIALS AND MARKS

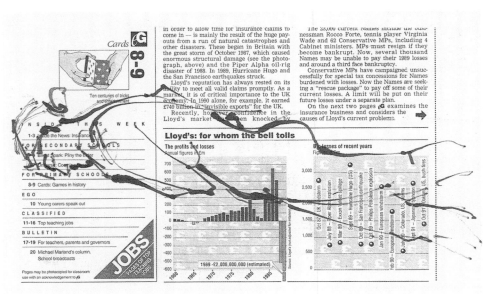

have happened on the backs of old coffee-stained envelopes.

2. A spiral-bound sketchbook to slip into a bag or pocket. Make sure it has a solid back.

3. A reasonable selection of cartridge paper. It ranges in tone from stark white through gray to warm cream. The texture can be satiny smooth or as rough as a plowed field. The smoother the texture, the less holding your paper will have. Soft pastels and charcoal will sit precariously on the surface, and will sometimes literally fall off and contaminate everything in the fall-out area. Very rough paper can trip you up and consume nibs and fracture pastels. This quality of paper would normally be stretched and worked over with a wet medium. Try to stick to the middle of the range; the extremes of rough and smooth are normally the province of the confirmed specialists.

4. Willow charcoal; the quality is often unpredictable but it lifts off easily.

5. Compressed charcoal. This is graded from hard to soft and is very black and dramatic.

6. White soft pastel for highlighting and editing.

7. Pencils, preferably B, 3B, 7B, which are at the soft end of the range. I find them more

BELOW

Viv Levy

Life-sized drawing made with a six-inch household brush and black and white emulsion.

You need to stand well back, use your whole arm and throw caution to the winds when wielding a decorating brush. The white paint is useful for obliterating mistakes, and a large roll of paper is essential, so that you can cut your surface to scale.

versatile and compassionate than the HB range, which is more suitable for the making of plans, maps and very accurate design work.

8. Black and white oil pastels. These are soluble in turpentine; you can produce interesting marks by laying down areas of oil or wax and washing over them with watercolor or ink.

9. Pen, nibs and ink.

10. A large putty eraser or a loaf of damp, sliced, white bread. The advantage of using pellets of bread to clean paper or to erase is that you have an endless clean supply. You will, however, have to contend with a mountain of carcinogenic crumbs and a pile of molding crusts.

11. Black and white household emulsion paint.

12. Small collection of brushes up to six inches, including cheap DIY variety.

13. Brown sticky tape for stretching paper. You do this by soaking the paper, laying it flat on a board and then sticking down all four sides with tape that has been run under the tap. By the time it has dried out the paper will be as tight as a drum and will take watercolor without bubbling.

14. Masking tape, for tacking down drawings, for masking off areas you want to leave white, or for achieving a hard edge.

15. Ozone friendly fixative spray.

16. Heavy-duty craft knife.

17. Fine-grained glass paper for shaping leads and graphite sticks.

RIGHT TOP
Organized mark-making on a smaller scale: (top) ink and wash manipulated with both edges of a flat brush; (above) pigment and wax applied and manipulated with a palette knife.

LEFT
Viv Levy
Plant
Drawing, made with charcoal, pastel, black and white paint, sprayed with water and belabored with sandpaper and sponges, 72 × 48 inches (184.3 × 122.9 cm)
A kind of organized dictionary of marks, early morning exercise in loosening up and banishing inhibitions.

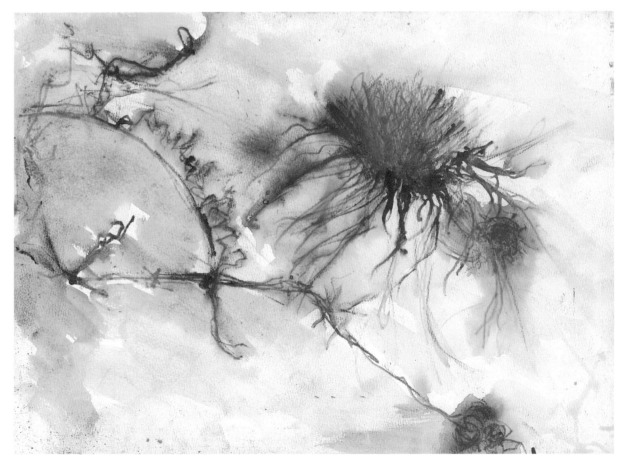

ABOVE
Viv Levy
Plant
Watercolor, applied with stick, pastel and wash, 12½ × 9¼ inches (32 × 23.7 cm)

18. A good-sized drawing board or a suitable substitute.

There are a million tools for free all around you: sticks, feathers, scraps of cloth and fingers (preferably yours). With a little ingenuity these can be transformed into efficient conveyors of ideas to paper.

The color you choose will depend on the subject you are looking at, whether you favor realism or a Fauvist flight into the imaginary. I used to lose control when I came across mouth-watering displays of colored materials. I have now, almost, managed to keep my hands off and buy only what is needed for the job in hand; over the years I have built up an awesome spectrum without going broke.

Making the First Mark

Nothing is more intimidating than a clean sheet of paper and a hoard of brand new materials. Break the spell and try everything out. You can learn to control the mark you make and to choose when to use it. Don't just accept the given point of a new pencil, tailor it to your needs. Expose the lead with a craft knife; a pencil sharpener will give you a universal point, excellent for applying make up or for drawing up plans, but useless if you want a varied subtly textured line. Don't be afraid of breaking charcoal to find a new line or of shaving it onto the surface to find another texture. See what happens when you spray the face of your drawing with water, how lines bleed, colors merge . . . Exploit accidents and do not allow them to paralyze you.

For your first project, make a dictionary of marks and annotate it. Try out every combination of the treasure trove of materials you have accumulated on as many sheets of paper as necessary: Chinese drawing ink swooshed onto tissue paper with a large brush; HB pencil missing the point on expensive hand-made watercolor paper; extra soft compressed charcoal dissolving and spreading, almost edible, on drenched newspaper; etc., etc.

Learn to enjoy your materials, not to fight with them. These are your potential allies. Find out about them, don't blame them retrospectively for your lack of judgment. Make your own index of possibilities.

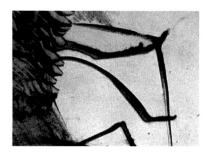

BELOW
Dictionary of marks

Pen and ink with nib at varying angles

Rubbed compressed charcoal

Black oil pastel with turps wash

Soft graphite

Overlay of white watercolor applied with palette knife

Black soft pastel

White masking fluid

HB pencil mark removed with eraser

HB pencil at an angle

Pen and ink

Feather and ink

White wax ink wash dropped on

Willow charcoal

Ink wash with white oil pastel

Block of black soft pastel applied with twisting motion

Compressed charcoal

3. Planning the Page

Placing the Figure on the Page

You have identified your model and the scene is set. You have rigged up a drawing board and fixed your paper to it, making sure that it is the right way up. Now plan the page, aiming to include the whole figure on the page. There are those who can never find a suitable piece of paper to accommodate their drawings. This is bad planning and if you allow it to happen, you will find yourself accepting compromises after the event. If you start out with the intention of drawing an enlarged detail, by all means do so, but if your original strategy was to draw the whole subject then plan the page accordingly; don't end up with a headless torso or minus the feet.

Aim to use the whole page, filling the space at your disposal; we will deal with the subtle stage management and manipulation of space once you are confident enough simply to draw what is in front of you.

Now spend time just looking and drawing in air. You may feel foolish gesticulating in a

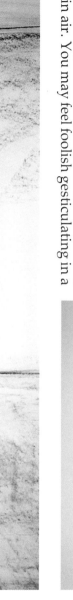

LEFT
Viv Levy
Model Clutching Cushion
Charcoal and pastel.
The model is firmly clamped to a huge cushion center page; the foot appears disproportionately large as it shoots forward toward me.

LEFT BELOW
Viv Levy
Model Asleep
Charcoal and pastel.
The bed she lies on and the verticals behind her are drawn in and operate as yardsticks to place her on the page. Get these right or they will send the whole drawing out of kilter.

TOP NEAR RIGHT
Viv Levy
Small Dog
8b pencil, 2⅜ × 4 inches (6.1 × 10.2 cm)
A very obvious example of someone who fits perfectly into a rectangle. I have isolated him in the middle of a landscape format to emphasize his lack of stature.

TOP FAR RIGHT
Viv Levy
Skeletal drawing 9½ × 12½ inches (24.3 × 32 cm)

RIGHT
Mike Winstone
Torso
Charcoal.
Deliberate study of part of the figure, planned to occupy the whole page.

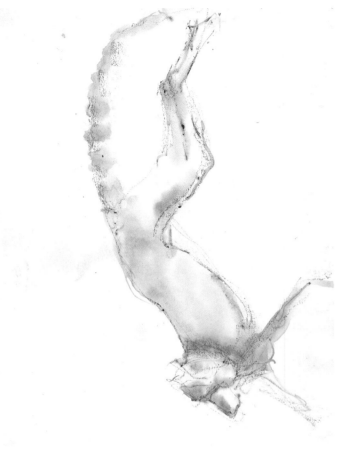

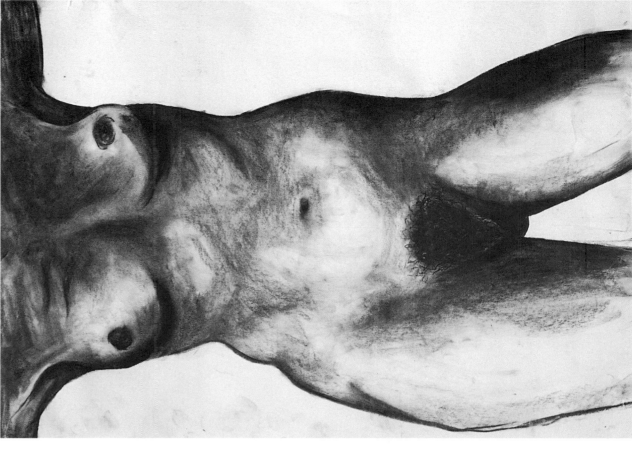

vacuum – this is what cameramen do when they are lining up a shot – but the practice run is a pause for thought, an opportunity to look again and to loosen up the arm. You may think you know your model very well, but it may be someone you see every day, but over-familiarity really does breed contempt. Without looking again or resorting to generalizations, (he has eye like Paul Newman's, a silken coat), try to describe, in words, the subject you are about to draw. Write it down if it helps you to formulate your thoughts. Now look again and see how useful your description was. How much notice had you really taken? Our ultimate aim when drawing is to find visual metaphors to accurately and sparingly describe the model, but you must first make sure that your seeing is meticulous.

If you are in any doubt about the mechanics of the pose, walk around and look at different views until you are sure that you understand it.

Mapping the Figure

Are there any verticals or horizontals in the picture? If so, establish them on the page, if not, either use the edges of the paper as a guide, or draw a faint cross down the center of the page; you now have a device with which to judge all the diagonals. Visualize the overall shape which is going to contain your model, square, rectangle, triangle, oval or circle, and place it on the drawing, bearing in mind its relationship to the established verticals and horizontals. Find the center.

Plot the dynamics, the famous diagonals. It is rare for any living thing to slip naturally into a symmetrical pose or to grow vertically and conveniently toward the ceiling, sprouting branches at regular intervals. There will be a swing of the hips, a tilt of the head, a twist of the spine, a stretch toward the sun; look out for this.

By now you should have a rudimentary map and be out of danger of falling off the

Expanding Your Plan

page or mislaying any limbs. Start plotting your way around your map. Look for useful reference points and punctuate the plan by placing the navel, the nipples, a bud, or any other strategically placed feature which will help you to see the way, checking their relative positions. Make sure that what you are seeing is physically possible; when in doubt, get into the pose yourself and feel your way around it. The spine of a human, or an animal, flows in a line from the skull to the coccyx, or the end of a tail; it cannot whizz around bends or break off mid-back to reappear behind an ear. The spine holds us up and cannot take leave of its moorings to wind up glued to a thigh or to the left or right of a shoulder blade. A front view has a center of gravity which is also governed by the position of the spine. Remember that one phenomenon affects another and you must be aware of the whole. If you are unable to see it from your view, get up, walk around and check it out.

The same general rules apply when you are tackling a plant. It will have a central stalk or trunk, branches reaching out at irregular intervals, buds pushing through, flowers emerging. Nothing is stuck on, everything is growing out of something else. Allow your drawing to grow in the same way. These are not dead things; look for their structure, keep them alive on the page.

Move, with a relaxed hand and arm, around your map, filling in information. Stand back from your work and make sure the proportions are correct. Don't at this stage get seduced by detail and decoration. You may be fascinated by a set of alluring eyelashes, an eccentric hairstyle or the tracery of veins, but resist the temptation to concentrate on them now. You may well be attaching them to absurdly spindly bodies, or using them as a good excuse not to include the feet.

Pin your subject down into context. There is always gravity; people and things do not float around in mid-air. Don't just plonk your model on the flat surface of the paper with no attempt to set him/her in space or to connect to the round. If your model is sitting, show us the seat of the chair, if standing indicate the floor. Shadows and reflections can also be exploited to establish your subject in the real world.

Don't be afraid of measuring. Unless your seeing is particularly acute, you can't always rely on instinct to get things right. Hold a pencil, or straight edge, at the end of an extended arm, at eye level. Don't bend your arm or change your eye level or you will get conflicting information. Close one eye and, with the tip of the pencil lined up with the item you want to check, slide your thumb up

or down until you find the opposite edge of the item, as if you were operating a slide rule. Take this measurement and check it against another section of the drawing; is truth stranger than fiction? You KNOW that a greyhound has a long muzzle but if he is pointing at you, nose on, it APPEARS short. You are getting a foreshortened view which you may find difficult to believe. Don't confuse what you know with what you see. If you simply cannot accept a degree of foreshortening, measure and check it against something you do understand, the corner of a room or the line of a shelf.

To survive these preliminary stages, make lots of drawings on cheap paper. Don't get bogged down with a time-consuming masterpiece but try things out; you can't do everything at once. Don't take on the responsibility of expensive paper which you will be afraid to ruin; you are allowed to make mistakes as long as they are profitable. Pin your work up at the end of the day and try honestly to assess your virtues as well as your faults. Don't chuck things out, they may look different tomorrow.

LEFT
Viv Levy
Quince
Pencil, 8 × 5⅝ inches (20.5 × 14.4 cm)
In bed, drawing my dog on the bed. His nose, up close, protruding upside down from the duvet is as large as a paw waving in the air.

BELOW LEFT
Viv Levy
Nude Asleep

BELOW
Viv Levy
Hassid
Pencil, 9 × 6¼ inches (23 × 16 cm)

RIGHT
Dido Crosby
Movement
Pen and ink, 16¼ × 11½ inches (41.6 × 29.4 cm)

4. Believing the Evidence of Your Eyes

We often take perverse delight in making life more difficult for ourselves than it really is. Everything in this section may seem glaringly obvious, but it is very often the 'obvious' that holds the key to success. We ignore or overlook it as we rummage around looking for higher, more challenging fences to hurdle. The simple message is LOOK before you leap.

Your most valuable assets for drawing are your eyes. The importance of looking and believing in what you see cannot be overstressed. Seeing is your business; you must spend time looking and know what to look for. I am bombarded with excuses from students too impatient to stop and absorb this advice, as they stare, disbelieving and furious, at the fruits of their, very real, labors. There is something wrong with their spectacles, the light is bad, they have a

blinding hangover, they find the model unsympathetic, they were being creative with the truth, they are living in a parallel universe.

You are at the beginning of a journey and your main concern should be recognizing and then avoiding bad habits. Your unique creativity, your need to make something more than a mere representation or decoration, and to include your emotions, will be fulfilled when you are less taken up with technical problems, when the co-ordination of your eyes, hands and brain is automatic. For the time being discipline is the byword to avoid disappointment and frustration. The mistakes you make early on in a drawing may seem insignificant at first, but unless you sort them out on the spot, if you try to get away with them, they will haunt the rest of the way and overwhelm the end

BELOW
Viv Levy
Reclining Nude
Charcoal and pastel.
This is a drawing that went wrong early on in the proceedings. In trying to salvage it I added layer upon layer of slightly off information. The result is overworked, overloaded and under-observed.

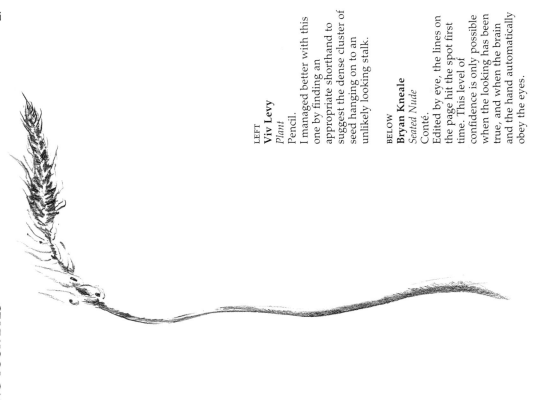

LEFT
Viv Levy
Plant
Pencil.
I managed better with this one by finding an appropriate shorthand to suggest the dense cluster of seed hanging on to an unlikely looking stalk.

BELOW
Bryan Kneale
Seated Nude
Conté.
Edited by eye, the lines on the page hit the spot first time. This level of confidence is only possible when the looking has been true, and when the brain and the hand automatically obey the eyes.

result. It is virtually impossible to pull off a convincing camouflage job if your looking was superficial and mistaken at the outset. The resulting drawing is a shambles of botched decisions. Do not accept approximations of the truth. We all have blind spots, but they have more to do with the inability of our brains to cope with the unwelcome surprises that our eyes have correctly registered. Holding on to images based on preconceptions is a form of indifference to that which is 'other'.

There are forms you may never have guessed at, let alone invented, until you start drawing. The more you draw, the more selective your vision will become. You will be able to identify the essence and edit the superfluous.

Try talking to yourself as you look; by explaining what you see you will make the subject more visible. Use your eyes and your mind's eye. Write down two or three observations about the model. Not 'it is green', 'it is big', 'she is beautiful'; although these statements may well be true, they are not specific enough to be of any use. Try variations on comments such as 'this person has a particularly long spine', 'the posture of a dancer', 'a quirky carriage of the head'. A plant may have particularly dense foliage: how do you suggest this without painstakingly drawing each and every leaf? (Refer to your dictionary of marks.) Now make your drawing about the specific observations you have written down. Get your mind and your eyes working in tandem; this co-operation will clarify your vision and lead you to your next move.

Keep your critical faculties on red alert. If you find it hard to assess your own work, try looking at it in a mirror or turning it upside down; try anything to find a different view. Try masking a section of your drawing with your hand or with another sheet of paper. This will help you to isolate problems and to deal with them without the pleasant distraction of the bits you are impressed with; it is quite possible that the unmasking of the good bits will reveal a need for more drastic surgery.

There is a tradition in Japanese painting, a ritual that elegantly describes the attention you owe to your eyes and mind before you start. The paper is spread on the floor. The ink is calmly and slowly mixed in a bowl by your side, with a rythmic, circular movement of the hand and arm, a kind of meditation. The subject is contemplated, summoned into the head, imprinted on the mind. When it is ready it is projected on to the page. The loaded brush comes out of the bowl, the stroke begins outside the paper, continues through the drawing space and projects beyond. The result is a loose, confident, moving line: drawings as full of peace as they are suggestive of life.

Teaching Yourself to Look

There is an exercise to improve your ability to hold on to what you see for long enough to transfer it to the page. Look at the subject carefully and critically, both its overall form and the detail of individual parts, for as long as it takes you to think that you have memorized it. Then close your eyes and see it again, burned on to the inside of your eyelids, and hold it there. Imagine that your eyelids are cinema screens and your mind is playing on to them the image you have just shot. Open your eyes and project that image on to a piece of paper you have at the ready. Draw around the image and fill in as much detail as you can, and compare your drawing to the real thing; how close is it to the 'held' impression? If you are miles off the mark, this suggests you were not looking hard enough

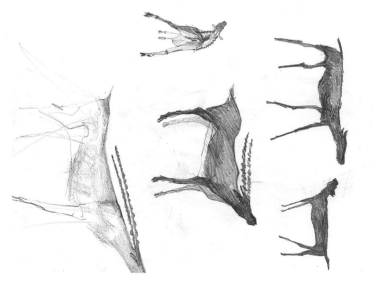

LEFT
Dido Crosby
Studies at the Zoo
Pencil

BELOW
Utagawa Kunisada (1786-1865)
Preparatory sketch for *Genji* series

RIGHT
Dido Crosby
Standing Nudes
Pencil
Looking for the essentials of the pose.

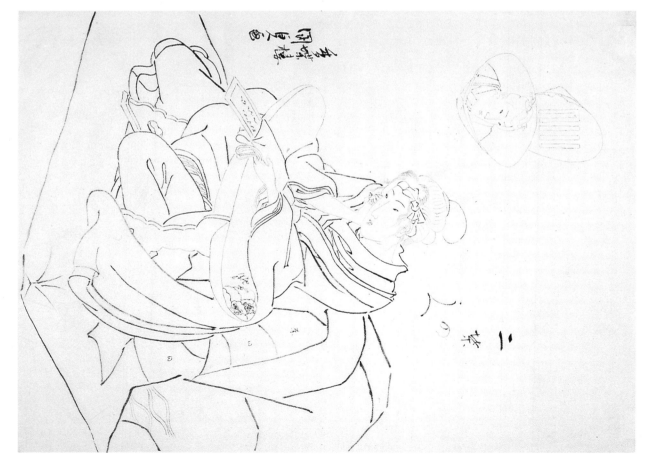

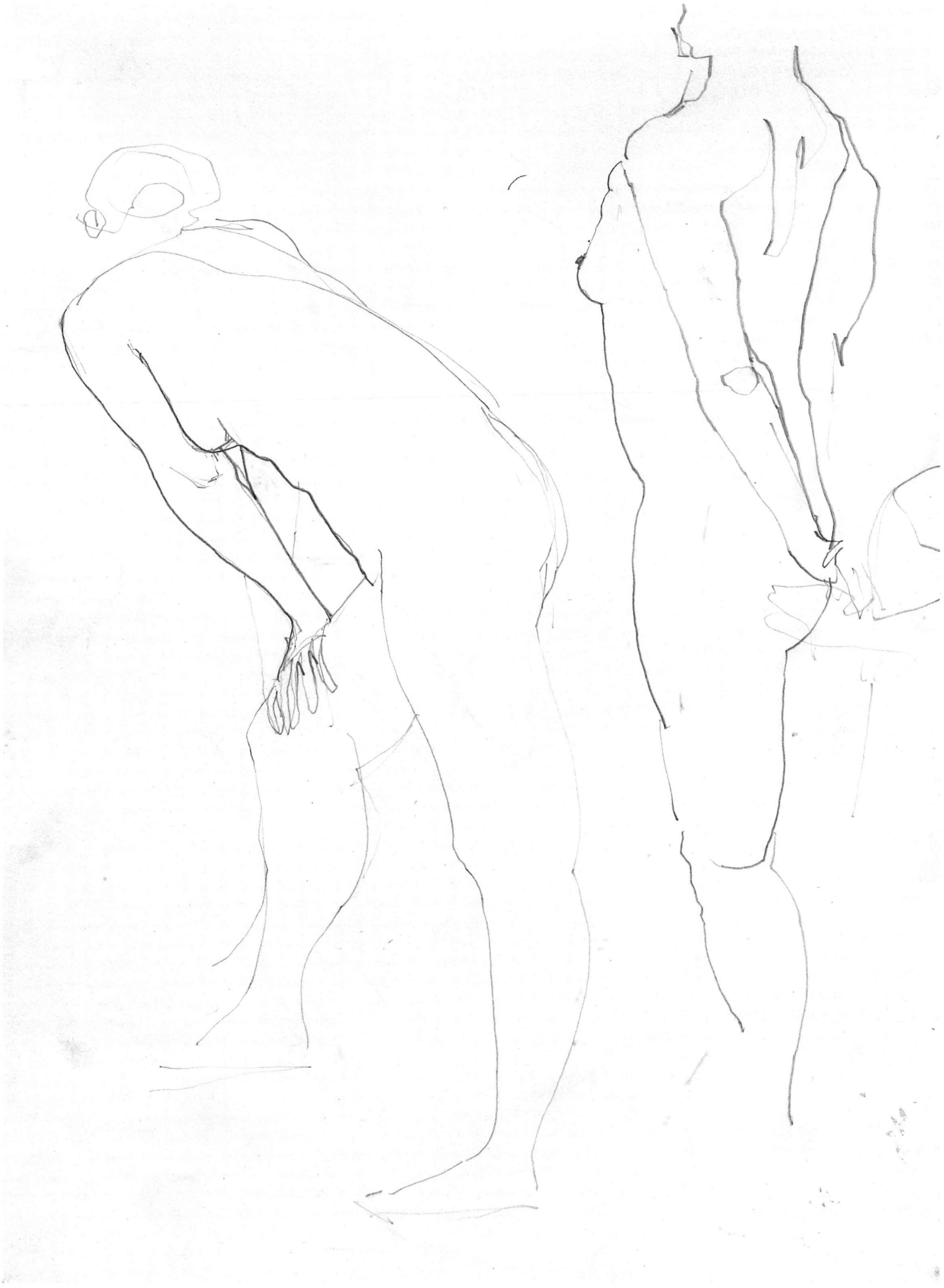

and you only registered a generalized blur in the first place. You need to train your eyes to see more clearly and your mind to absorb and retain more detail. Keep trying again until you begin to feel satisfied with the results.

Another way of testing the acuteness of your seeing and the extent of your concentration is to pretend that you are describing a close but absent friend to a stranger, and then to draw as you describe. Or pick the most familiar object in your life, something that you use or look at every day, and draw it from memory. Take the drawing to the object. How do they compare? Be critical of your performance; don't let yourself off lightly. Taking the easy path now will only undermine you in the long run.

By now you should be becoming aware of the lacunae in your looking, of how much you take for granted, the amount of vital information you miss even when you think you are in full command of your faculties.

I remain shameless about repeating the order to LOOK. Looking is a prerequisite to drawing, it shouldn't be a tedious grind. If you find it so, it is probably because you are bored with the subject matter, you have looked and seen nothing to persuade you to repeat the experience. If this is the case, accept it, change the pose or find something else to draw. Don't fear mistakes; as long as you learn to recognize them, and remember to avoid them next time, you will be winning. Train your eye to suspend judgment and disbelief. Your intuition and imagination will eventually come into play but they are not substitutes for looking. You are sure to have a few happy accidents to sweeten the pill; remember how they occurred and employ them to your advantage. Chance should be your friend.

ABOVE LEFT
John Dougill
Ink and bleach, 16¼ × 8 inches (41.6 × 20.5 cm)
This is all you need to know about the pose: hands on waist, swing of the hips, braced leg. Although the medium is unpredictable the artist hasn't panicked; he has tamed it and exploited the staining to tell all at speed.

ABOVE RIGHT
John Dougill
Wash on page of exercise book.
The figure lives and moves in two strokes of the brush.

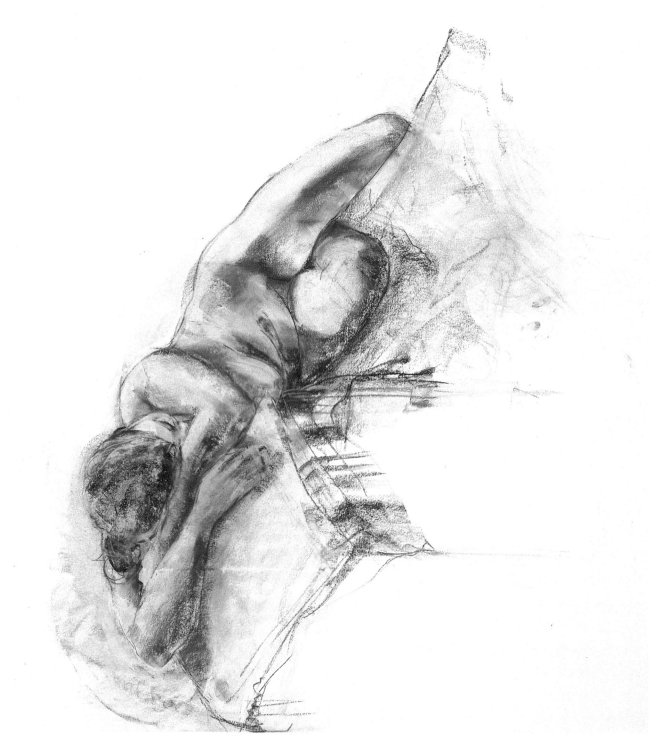

BELIEVING YOUR EYES

ABOVE
Viv Levy
Model with Cushion

LEFT
Viv Levy
Model Asleep

5. Exercises and Devices

Uses of Anatomy

You cannot operate by other people's rules. I believe that the time to resort to the anatomy manuals is when you know what you are looking for. Looking up a word in a dictionary is a huge problem if you are ignorant of the first letter.

The Renaissance was a time of change and discovery; artists were at the forefront of research into anatomy. Nowadays information is easy to come by. There are museums and medical establishments brimming with skeletons and flayed figures, there are publications like *Gray's Anatomy* (we all religiously purchased copies at art school and were so exhausted by the time we had carried them home that they remain unopened to this day). Take what you need, don't become saturated with facts that may hinder your seeing. Our external features often belie the underlying armatures. It would be neat if we could divide the world into species, learn the mechanics, flesh them out, and in so doing breathe life and individuality into our creations. Shades of Frankenstein. Don't rely on dispossessed theories. By all means read about proportion but don't accept other people's equations verbatim, check them out for yourselves; the proportion of classical form is true to experienced proportion.

'From the eyebrow to the junction of the lip with the chin, from the angle of the jaw to where the ear joins the temple, will be a perfect square.' – Leonardo

'. . . For our eye is cunning, and is learned without rule by long use, as little lads speak their vulgar tongue without grammar rules. But I gave him rules, and sufficient reason to note and observe: as that the little man's head being commonly as great as the tall man's, then of necessity the rest of the body must be the less in that same scantling. A little man also short legs and thighs in comparison to his bulk of body or head; but though the head be as great as the tall man's yet shall his form and face and countenance be far otherwise easy enough to discern. The tall man hath commonly low shoulders,

long shanks, thighs, arms, hands and feet, wherewith our eye is so commonly acquainted that without rule to us known, it knoweth straight. But if an ill painter come which will make a child's head as little for his body as a tall man's (a child is but four times the length of his face, and a man ten times more) or his eye as little for his face as a man's, or his nose as great, I will not take

BELOW
Viv Levy
Charcoal and pastel
What is nearest is largest.

RIGHT
Dido Crosby
Model on the Move
Ink, 16¼ × 11½ inches (41.6 × 29.4 cm)
The easels remain constant, the model moves.

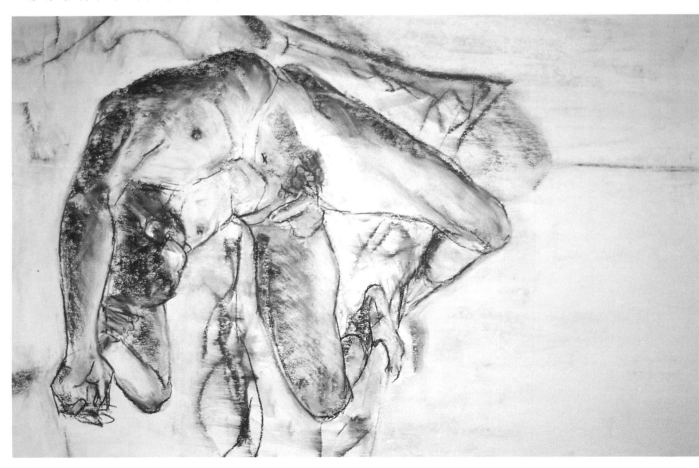

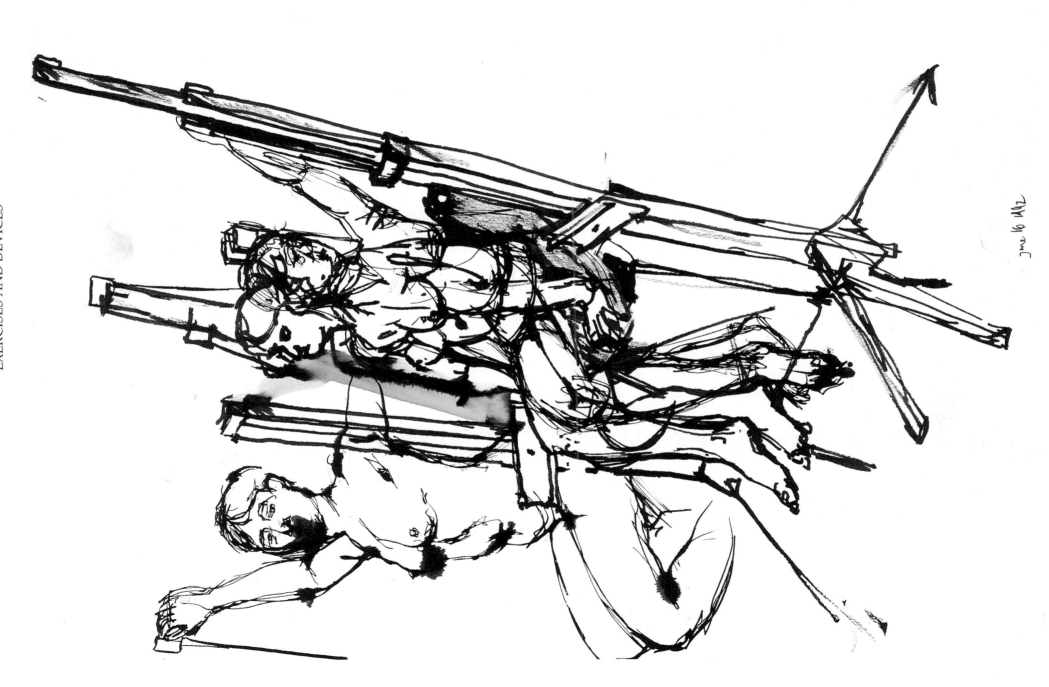

upon me to know his tall man for a dwarf.' – Nicholas Hilliard

Well, there you are; some eminent advice for you to try out.

These exercises are designed to change your looking habits, to give you a framework to fall back on and a yardstick to measure up to. You will find that some of these devices will help you to achieve dramatic results but they are not a guaranteed recipe for the perfect drawing. Once you see how to render certain 'effects', you must be prepared to take risks and not just settle for the security of style.

The Model in Perspective The most sensible way to understand perspective is to remember that the thing closest to you is, comparatively, the largest. Look at the model and find the nearest point to you, then look for the point furthest away. Measure and compare. If you have chosen to tackle a foreshortened view, for instance a sitting pose with a foot stretched out at eye level, the underside of the big toe may appear to be as large as the head; measure and check and believe. 'What's nearest is largest'; allow this instruction to follow you around through all your drawings.

Exercise 1 Set up the subject matter or pose the model, then set up your drawing so that you will be working with your back to the subject. This will force you to make a conscious move to look long and hard in order to gather enough information to take to your drawing. It will stop you from snatching quick glances and from accepting approximate messages. Every time you need information you must turn your entire body

LEFT
School of Leonardo
Leda, c.1510
Red chalk, 10⅞ × 6 ⅞ inches (27.5 × 17 cm)
Look at the ways of tackling hair. You can almost feel the dense coils of thick hair in this exceptionally baroque coiffure, but the drawing remains uncluttered as it contrasts floating tendrils and ribbed plaits with the stillness and serenity of the face.

RIGHT
Leonardo da Vinci
Head
Proportions of the Human Head
Silverpoint on blue prepared paper, 8¾ × 6 inches (21.3 × 15.3 cm)
Check this out for yourself. See how little space the features occupy in comparison to the rest of the head; take special note of the position of the ears.

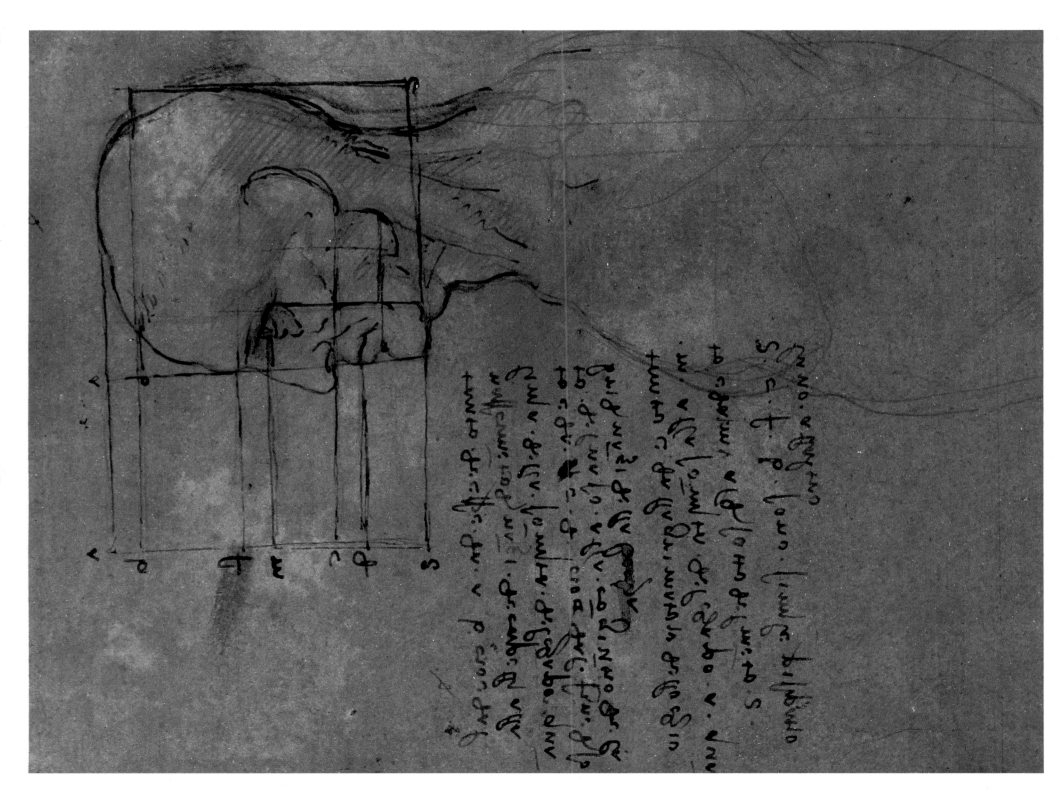

around with a specific problem in mind, target that problem only, solve it, and take the answer back to the page. If you look for too much information at once, you will only retain a blurred impression of what you have seen. Your drawing will always tell you what to look for on the next turn. Resist cheating by angling for swift squints over your shoulder; you could put your neck out and will anyway be defeating the whole purpose of the exercise. The object is to force you to look, to teach you what to look for and never to accept nonchalantly the first thing you think you have seen.

Exercise 2 Make a set for your model to work in; by the way, you are allowed to turn around for this one. Make sure that your set includes a horizontal and a vertical. A large window, mirror or door frame will do, as long as you leave yourself enough room to distance yourself and get a good view of the whole picture. Draw the horizontal and the vertical, making sure they are properly placed on the page; these lines are your frame. Now look for the negative spaces between them and your model; the shapes that occur outside your subject, if they are accurately observed, will reveal the subject to you. This is a good ploy to capture moving figures; the inanimate components are constant reference points in a changing scene. Get your model to move every five minutes and draw the changing shapes that occur between the model and the frame. Work the drawings one on the top of another. Step back and see if you have made sense enough of the movement to reproduce the poses yourself.

Be prepared; this is going to be a long drawing. Make sure that your model is comfortable, that your animal is out for the count. You are to draw everything in the room but the model. The minute you encounter the silhouette of the subject, stop and go back to an adjacent portion of the room. Don't draw a line around the subject, it will appear of its own accord once you have dealt with everything else. You will end up with a ghostly presence; the empty space on your page will describe the model exactly, as long as you have accurately observed the containing landscape.

Both these exercises help to dispel the panic and fear that people often experience the first time they draw from life, simply by getting you to look elsewhere and allowing the figure to emerge, unbidden, out of the backdrop. Many students who are perfectly competent with structured objects give up in

despair when they try to embrace and reproduce the human form. The planes, curves and angles of the body are beyond them because they are unable to perceive them with the same logical intelligence that they apply to something inanimate. Removing the anxiety factor is half the battle.

When I was a student I fractured my right hand, I felt very sorry for myself and assumed that I would automatically be '*hors de combat*' until it healed. No such luck; I was ordered to stop wingeing forthwith and to use my left hand, which would not reproduce the ghastly misdemeanors of its mate. My first, reluctant and peevish attempts were shaky, tentative and highly embarrassing. Once I threw caution to the winds and gave up fighting, the bad habits programmed into the thinking hand vanished and the taste control switch flipped off, as I became preoccupied with finding a 'view' of the model that this unschooled hand could cope with. The goal, of course, is to get both halves of the brain working together, instinct and intellect conspiring to reveal all your talents. I now find that working with my left hand is a good trick to help me refocus, get me off automatic pilot, and shake and loosen me up when I have been concentrating very hard for too long and begun to fall back on habit rather than sight. Try it out; give the obedient hand a rest, the other one is a talented entertainer.

BELOW
Tiles on the kitchen floor; dog fitted on to the grid. Once you get the grid right you should be able to slot the image into it correctly, at speed.

RIGHT
David Annesley
Line drawing of dog made without looking at the paper, in one continuous line.

weapon. Your nose will now be effectively removed from the surface of your drawing; you will have a holistic rather than a close-up view and will be forced to use your whole arm, to make large, 'meant', marks to describe the model.

This is a technique that was once used in the theater, before the invention of projectors, to give an overview while painting backcloths. Huge drawings are impossible to visualize at close range. You can't be in two places at once, both the creator and the spectator, but by using a long-handled brush you can place yourself somewhere in the middle and find a vantage point to accommodate both appetites.

Exercise 3 There are always groans from my students, and a beeline for the nearest exit, when I announce the next project, but once you realize that it is possible and get stuck into it, you will begin to see why it was

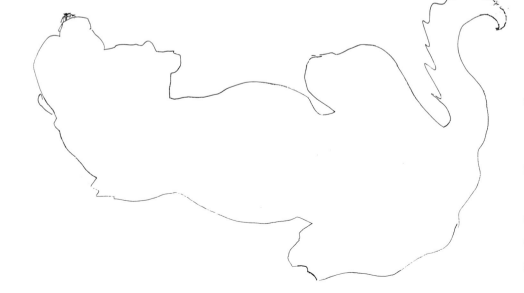

Gaining Control

Now that both hands, your brain and two eyes are warmed up, it is time to get them all working simultaneously on some more challenging projects.

Exercise 1 The first time you try this choose something simple and symmetrical to draw; for example a standing pose, legs braced, arms relaxed at the sides. Using both hands, a pencil in each, two different colors if you wish, start at the top of the page with both leads poised at the same point, then, slowly, very slowly, draw them apart to caress the contours of the figure. Keep both hands moving all the time, don't jerk your way around the drawing but keep the movement slow and smooth. You will find that your hands want to mirror each other, and you will have to concentrate hard in order to get them to describe the two sides of the picture simultaneously: instinct and control working hand in hand.

Exercise 2 Another way to confuse control and to find a constant overview of your subject is to work at arm's length, to prescribe a distance from your drawing. Find a stick, a straight one, about three foot long, and attach a piece of charcoal to one end. Your position, from which you are not to veer, is at the other end of this long-handled

worth staying. You are about to draw the model upside down. I am not, for one moment suggesting that you should stand on your head, nor am I asking you to do a conventional drawing and reverse it later. Establish the floor at the top of the page, plant the feet firmly upon it and continue downward until you reach the head at the bottom of the drawing. This is not gratuitous torture; it is meant to persuade you that your eyes can reason. When you do, eventually, return the drawing to its formal stance, don't scream and make intemperate adjustments before you have compared it with the innocent 'right way up' world, and rationalized your former brain work.

Exercise 4 A terracotta sculpture is made by laying one roll of clay on top of another until you arrive at the completed, hollow, form. In order to predict the finished form you need to be able to think and visualize in cross-section. You have to be aware of three dimensions and to be able to understand the shapes through the center of a form. Try to imagine that you have taken a saw to your long-suffering model, and proceed to slice sections through him/her/it (i.e. through the head, from the tip of an ear, through the nose to the jaw, straight through the middle at the waist, or diagonally from shoulder to thigh). Draw these imaginary sections as though you were looking down on them. With these drawings in front of you, turn away from the model and reconstitute the pose from your notes.

Exercise 5 Here are a couple of devices to warm the hearts of the scientists among you. Firstly, how to make the perfect drawing, cold and correct. You will need a rectangular piece of card, roughly 9×5 inches. From the middle of this cut a smaller rectangle 4×3 inches, so that you are left with a substantial frame. The inside edges of this frame will correspond exactly to the size of your drawing; trace around them on to the paper. Divide and mark out these edges at half-inch intervals; the intervals on the card must match up precisely to those on the paper.

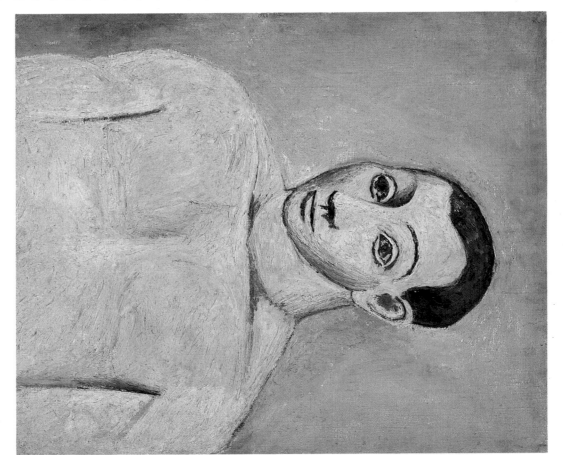

ABOVE
Picasso
Self-Portrait (1906)
Oil on canvas.
Unmistakably Picasso. He has made everything of his unique features and leaves us to believe the odd connection between neck and anonymous torso.

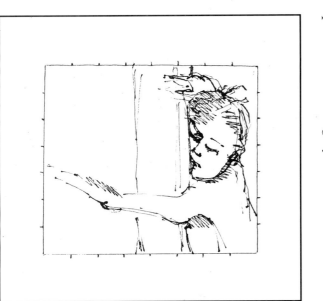

FAR LEFT
Cardboard frame to view through.

LEFT
Your drawing: same dimensions as the inside perimeter of frame.

Clip the cardboard frame to your drawing board, in alignment with the drawn rectangle and at eye-level, so that you are able to view the subject through it without writhing and squirming. Close one eye and focus through the frame as if it were the viewfinder of the camera. Using the corresponding measurements along the edges as reference points, fit the drawing into the frame; what you see is what you get, so stick to the rules and there will be no room for creative meanderings from the truth.

Exercise 6 For this you will have to draw out a grid on the floor. You may have a ready-made grid of carpet or lino tiles but if not, measure it out in masking tape. The squares should be about a foot square and the whole area should be large enough to accommodate the model lying flat out. Begin by drawing the grid without the model. This is more difficult, and will require much more time, than you may initially think, as you

will be looking down on the grid at an angle and seeing it in perspective. Take the time to accomplish an accurate drawing, as this stage is crucial to the ultimate success of the exercise. When you have finished, ask your model to lie prone on the grid and superimpose this image on to your drawing, using the receding squares as a guide.

These two last exercises require a pragmatic approach; stay calm. I'm not an exponent of the cool measured drawing, I don't believe in seeing the model as part of the furniture, but I think it is important to prove to yourself that you are capable of seeing in a mechanical way, even if you dislike the computerized results. This sort of concentration is a way of tuning and honing the eye; the mechanical processes enable you to set visual traps, and give you a yardstick with which to study the enmeshed results and make sense of what you are looking at on paper.

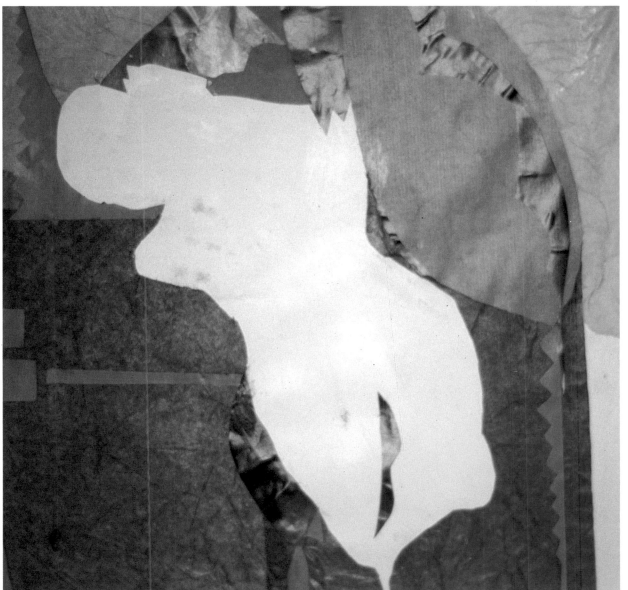

6. Line

' . . . The principal part of painting or drawing after the life consisteth in the truth of the line; as one sayeth in a place that he hath seen the picture of Her Majesty in four lines very like: meaning by four lines but the plain lines, as he might well have said in one line.'

— Nicholas Hilliard

'If a sculpture could be a line drawing, then speculate that a line drawing removed from its paper bond and viewed from the side would be a beautiful thing.'

— David Smith

The apparent speed and ease of the spare and eloquent line drawing should not be misinterpreted. Its simplicity is deceptive, and is certainly not synonymous with laziness or lack of time and concentration; on the contrary. You need to evolve a reductive technique and learn to edit with your eyes before you begin to draw, you need to grasp the essentials of the subject and to render them with economy, with line alone. Matisse talked of making drawings out of 'lightness and joy which never let anyone suspect the labor that they cost'.

Line does not have to be a sterile, constant mark, the boring track of the biro. You should already have found some rich and varied examples of line for your dictionary of

ABOVE
David Annesley
Self-Portrait
Graphite, 15½ × 11½ inches
(39.7 × 29.4 cm)
Self portrait without the
help of a mirror. This is an
astonishing likeness.

LEFT
Rembrandt
Study of Two Pigs
Loose notation of a
relatively small amount of
information and yet the
beasts are there, heavy,
smelling of good earth and
they make me smile in
recognition.

LINE

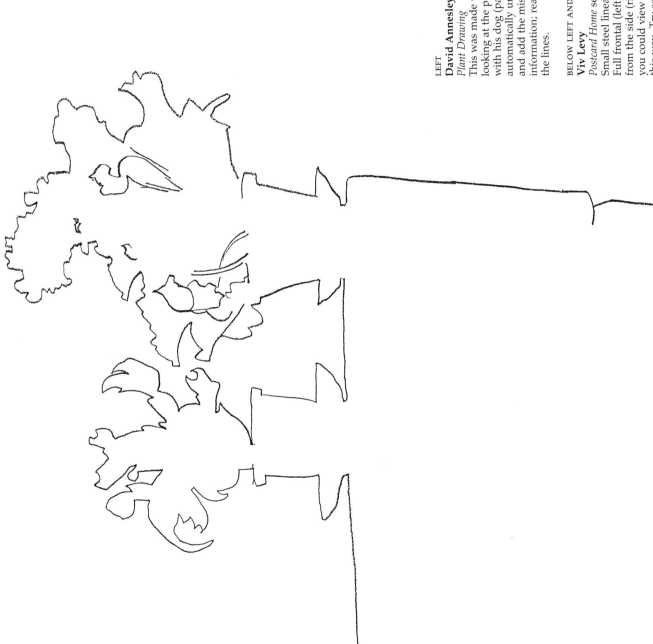

LEFT
David Annesley
Plant Drawing
This was made without looking at the paper. As with his dog (page 37), you automatically understand and add the missing information; read between the lines.

BELOW LEFT AND RIGHT
Viv Levy
Postcard Home series
Small steel linear sculpture. Full frontal (left) and seen from the side (right). If only you could view drawings this way. Try some wire drawings.

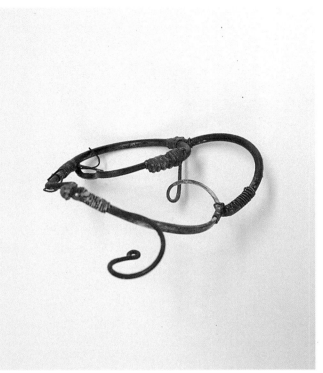

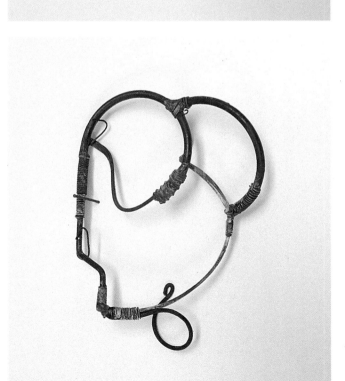

marks. Exploit a variety of materials and remain sensitive to their versatility. Think about what that glib phrase 'such a wonderful quality of line' really means. A line can be fragile or strong, pure and cold or sensual and loud, as long as it is pertinent to the character of the subject you are describing. Each line that you make should enhance and complement its neighbor and should not retrace or eradicate it. Your lines should sing; do not be tentative or stiff. Be prepared to make dramatic errors of judgment, and for your corrections and revisions to be exuberant and courageous; if a line is manifestly wrong the correction should be manifestly right, not a pale imitation of the mistake. Anxious scratchings and feeble stabbings, accompanied by vigorous rubbings out, do not lead to success.

A line is not a perimeter fence. It is not there to stop the insides from getting out, like skin; it is a device to make sense of what you are looking at on paper. Use it to delineate not to overstate. If you are trying to capture a moving figure, line is all you will have time for, with an eye like a camera on motor drive and the reactions of a young cat. Don't go back to recapture lost moments

Alexander Calder
The Circus, 1932
Pen and ink, 20¼ × 29¼
inches (51.8 × 74.9 cm)
This is a drawing, not a
photograph of a wire
sculpture. Calder was able
to perceive three
dimensions, and express
them with a single simple
line as if he were holding
the subject in his hand.

Viv Levy
Self-Portrait
Charcoal.
Arctic conditions made
speed an essential
prerequisite to making this
line drawing. It is
sometimes beneficial to
stack the odds against
yourself: a good ruse to
break bad habits.

after the event; if you were alert enough, your original shorthand should be sufficient to say it all.

Exercise 1 Pick your subject. Stare at it. Now find your way around it with one continuous line without looking at the paper. Keep looking at the model, keep drawing; if the subject moves, take the line on the same journey. Don't even think about sneaking a look at the paper or you will immediately start to make value judgements and adjustments. You are trying to get a loose feel for moving line, not to make a pretty drawing. Only look when you feel that this part of the drawing is finished, and then you may see if there are any very slight additions you can make to render it more 'visible'. Punctuate the silhouette with just enough information to make it identifiable; don't get involved with detailing all the hairs on a head or a tracery of vessels on a leaf. The indication of a spine or placement of a central stalk will do.

Exercise 2 Close your eyes and think about how it feels to be inside your head, as if you were pushing out toward the skin. With your eyes shut draw a self-portrait. For information use a remembered image of your-self and also use touch. Glide one hand over and around your face, draw the other one over the paper, draw what you feel in your body, use line, and don't panic about losing your place. Draw yourself full face and in profile. You will soon become familiar with the space on the page and to the sensation of being led by the line.

Alexander Calder made drawings exactly as if they were pieces of thin wire, as if he had flattened out his wire sculptures on the page. This exercise is greeted with rage and dismay: 'You're asking us to make sculpture and you're supposed to be teaching drawing.' David Smith described some of his linear sculptures as drawings in air. We are going to take a line for a walk into the third dimension, to get you to see that it is possible to 'speak' volume with line.

Exercise 3 Find a length of wire soft enough to manipulate in your hands and long enough to describe the figure in one line. You are not to make a matchstick person, animal or plant. This is not going to be an armature to be fleshed out with clay; the flesh will be implied with line. The line is going to pick up on the essentials of the pose, it is going to work backward and for-

ABOVE
Henri Matisse
Reclining Nude, 1927
Oil on canvas
Matisse kept the drawing of the model simple and threw her into sharp relief by painting in all the decorative pattern, clutter and color around her.

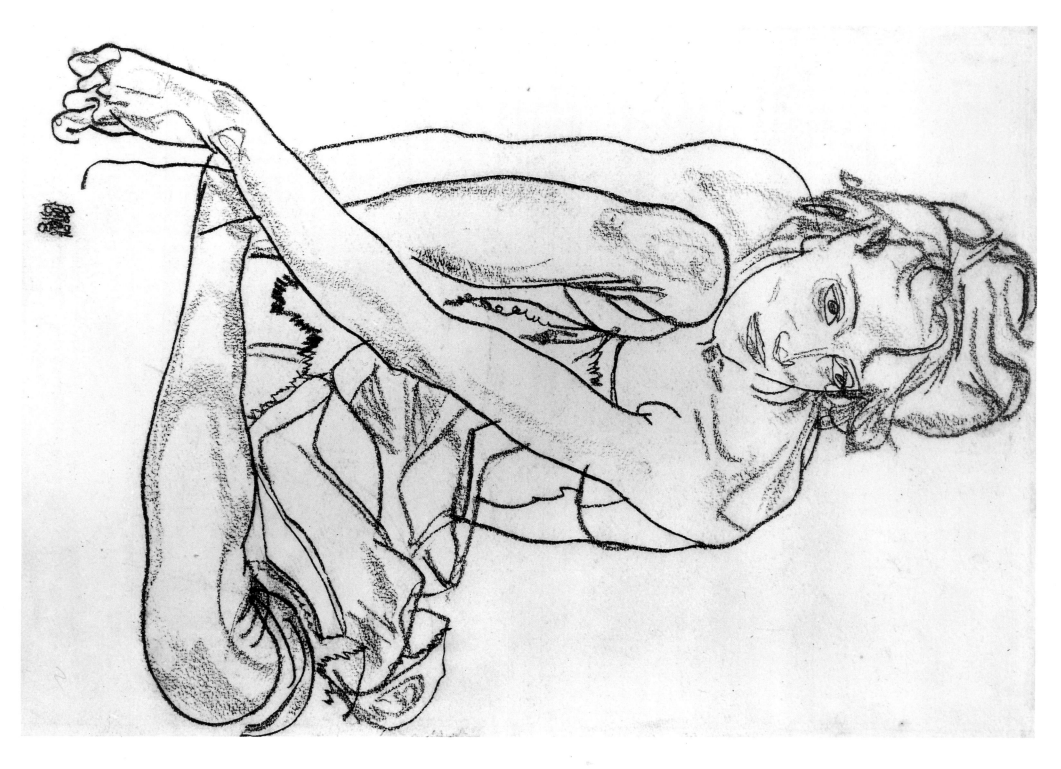

LINE

ward through it (see cross-sections), and not just around it so that you end up with some sort of ill-advised gingerbread person. Don't rush; look carefully and find the best place to start. You only have one line and it has a long way to travel. Don't be over ambitious with the scale or you'll end up ensnared in yards of tangled steel and an overwhelming desire to reach for the pliers; pliers are banned. Aim to make a piece that sits happily in the hand. When it is finished use it as a guide to make a line drawing of the same

pose. With this three-dimensional aid you should be able to understand the subject from every view, including a view from above and below. Don't insert lines that you failed to see in the original but adapt the ones that are there; stretch them and manipulate them on the page until you have a see-through reversable image made of drawn line. You should be aware of transferring the plasticity of the wire into the line on the page.

For the last three drawings your line has

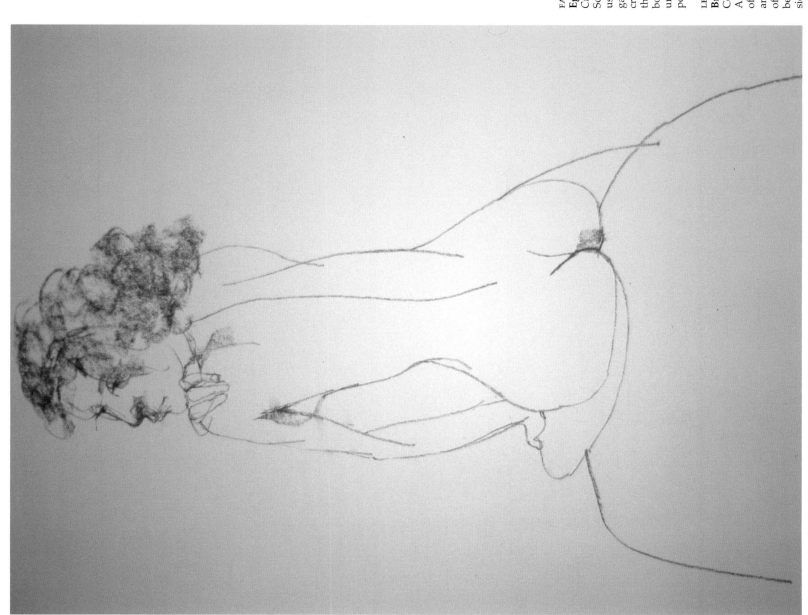

been 'given'; you have not been asked to be inventive with the quality of a changing line or to manipulate the section of a line. A line can move from thick to thin, from light to dark, from fast to slow. Start experimenting with a brush of the soft, flexible, tapering, Japanese drawing brush variety. Vary the feel of the line by the amount of pressure you exert or by changing the angle of the brush. Use drawing ink or a thin wash of color. Keep your touch light and your wrist loose. Look carefully and aim accurately; the medium is indelible and has an assertive presence. Take the plunge and make the drawing in a gesture. Be as theatrical as you

LEFT
Viv Levy
Seated Nude
Oil pastel and turpentine,
16¼ × 11½ inches (41.6 ×
29.4 cm)
Taking a line for a walk in a
soft medium extravagantly
tailored to my needs, and
softened further by dipping
the pastel in turps.

BELOW
Viv Levy
Caricature of a Cross Dog
Pencil, 4⅛ × 5½ inches
(10.6 × 14.1 cm)
He really was saying that. I
did him from memory after
a particularly bizarre
altercation with my dog in
the course of our morning
walk.

RIGHT
Viv Levy
Dog Chomping a Bone
Pencil
Part of a series of a dog
trying to extract the marrow
from a huge bone on
someone else's carpet. We
were talking throughout
these drawings, serenaded
by alarming crackings and
slurpings. Drawing by
proxy.

ABOVE
Bryan Kneale
Seated Nude
Conté, 16¼ × 11½ inches (41.6 × 29.4 cm)
This borders on caricature but avoids it by a hair's breadth. The model was clearly relaxed but you can feel the drawing willing her not to move for just one second longer. You can read the relative speed of the line as it travels from the shoulder, around the hand in the foreground and back, to recommence down the spine.

like, enjoy the freedom, the physical sensation, of the generous, live line. Make lots of these drawings on cheap newsprint until you feel you know the means and are able to surrender to them. You can be just as free with a line of charcoal or pastel, just remember not to accept prescribed marks dictated by the pristine point you found in the shop. Peel the paper off pastels so that you can reverse them on to their sides, shave or break charcoal until it gives you the line YOU want. If you are using pencil, expose a large expanse of lead on one face and use fine sandpaper to tailor the point to the required line. You should not be at the mercy of your materials; they are there to serve you. I often use sticks and splinters of wood instead of pens. I find them more versatile, as I can whittle or mash them into submission with no accompanying feelings of guilt.

It is very tempting to slip into caricature when you restrict yourself to drawing with line; to emphasize features without regard to the variety of the model. Try deliberately caricaturing the model: look for a feature, or features, to exaggerate, then do another version keeping what you originally saw under control and in proportion. There is a very fine dividing line between crude caricature and selective vision. Some people just can't resist crossing it; be sure of your motives.

The secret of a successful line drawing is in what you leave out. The frugal art of line is entirely pitiless. Enter into collaboration, a conspiracy, with the line and wait to see what the result will be.

7. Light

'The Light is either born here or, imprisoned, reigns here in freedom.'
– Inscription in the Archiepiscopal Chapel at Ravenna

Light is an essential prerequisite for seeing. Depending on the light source and the quality and quantity of light, form is either emphasized or flattened. Once you have grasped a simple logical system of understanding the laws of light and of investing a light source, you will have found a way of seeing that will enable you to understand and express form and mass.

All you need to know is that all surfaces perpendicular to a light source receive the same light value, while the more a surface is turned away from the light source the darker it becomes. Perspective and intensity of light work as well on a figure drawing as on a landscape.

Exercise 1 Having extolled the virtues of light, I am now going to ask you to make a drawing in the dark. If you have the means to black out a room during the hours of daylight, then do so, if not wait until darkness falls. As your eyes become accustomed to the dark, you will be able to discern your subject and can start to draw. Draw only what you are able to see, don't add prior information or rely on memory. As you progress you will be surprised at the extent of your seeing. Students complain that they are unable to see what they are doing to the page, let alone what is looming in the room. No bad thing; every decision you make will depend on your ability to force yourself to see; sloppy-looking invention or flashy decoration will not help. When you have plumbed the gloom for all it's worth, bring in one feeble light source. Start with one candle or the beam from a torch, and add information as it is relayed to you; gradually

LEFT
Georges Seurat
Seated Boy with Straw Hat,
1882
Conté crayon, 9½ × 12¼
inches (24.3 × 31.4 cm)
There is no line in this
drawing; it is created out of
patterns of light.

TOP RIGHT
Viv Levy
Irises
Pencil and graphite, 9½ ×
14 inches (24.3 × 35.8 cm)
These were standing
against the window, backlit
and irresistible. The dark
and light were not
substitutes for color; they
were the actual tones I was
seeing.

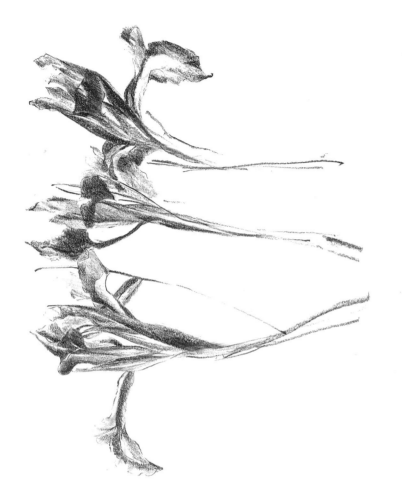

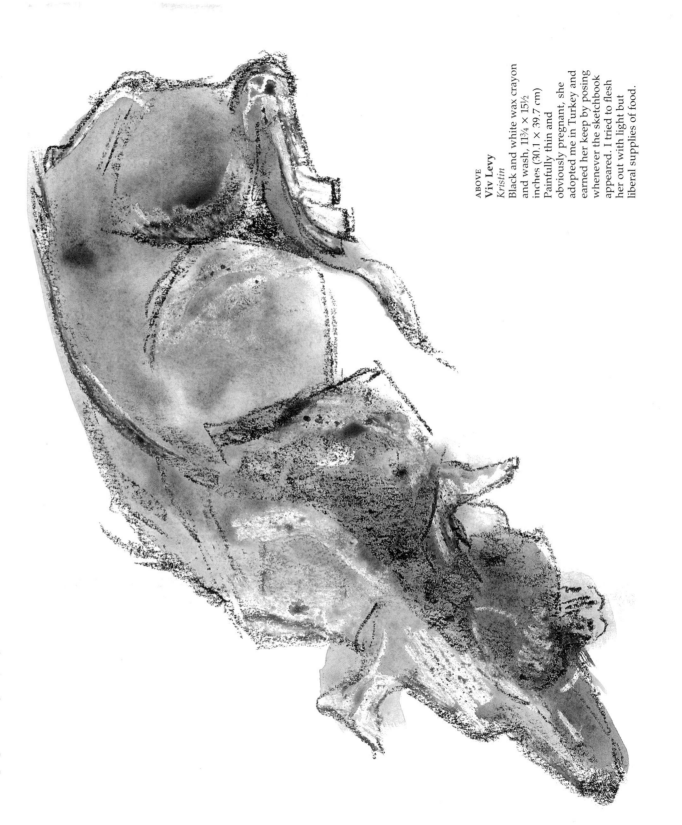

LIGHT

bring up more and more light. The more the light reveals to you, the more you will add to your drawing. Carry on until you are satisfied that you have seen and recorded enough.

Exercise 2 This next exercise also involves moving from dark to light. This time, though, it is your page that is going to start off dark and you will find the subject by removing pigment from the surface, by seeing the light. Set up your subject in a raking light, from one strong source, so that you are seeing highly contrasting areas of light and dark. Scour your paper with soft charcoal or graphite – a roughish surface will hold the pigment – until you have an even black page. Look for the lightest areas of the picture and remove them with a putty eraser or a handful of breadcrumbs. When you have mapped out the lightest areas, find the black, if necessary pushing more black into the page. Let your eye travel across the

ABOVE
Viv Levy
Kristin
Black and white wax crayon
and wash, 11¾ × 15½
inches (30.1 × 39.7 cm)
Painfully thin and
obviously pregnant, she
adopted me in Turkey and
earned her keep by posing
whenever the sketchbook
appeared. I tried to flesh
her out with light but
liberal supplies of food.

forms from one extreme to another and start to pick out the mid-tones. With the eraser in one hand and charcoal in the other, add and subtract until the image coheres. Don't use line; ban it altogether from this drawing. The image you are creating may seem difficult to read to begin with; you may find it mind-numbing trying to find your way around the figure unaided by line. Persevere. Stick to a search for the play of light, the abstract shapes it makes, and the subject will appear as if by magic.

Exercise 3 Set up a pale figure against a black backdrop. Shine an intense light on the scene from one source, so that you have a dramatic area of contrasting tones to look at. Don't confuse tone with color; the darkest shadows on the white will be as intense and as dark as those on the black, as long as they are receiving the same amount of light. Make the drawing by looking for the dark, leaving the light to fend for itself. Draw the abstract shapes created by the shadows and don't draw lines around the white bits. Have faith; they will still be there if you spot them in time and resist interfering with them. Obey natural laws. Line is a means of conveying form to paper; nature does not rely on it to display its wonders. Light is a natural phenomenon; to understand it, imitate the way it works, see how it reveals and conceals.

Exercise 4 Choose an even flat light; the drama of this scene will come from you. Imagine that you have a strong light emanating from the end of your nose, and that this is the only light source. Hold this imaginary

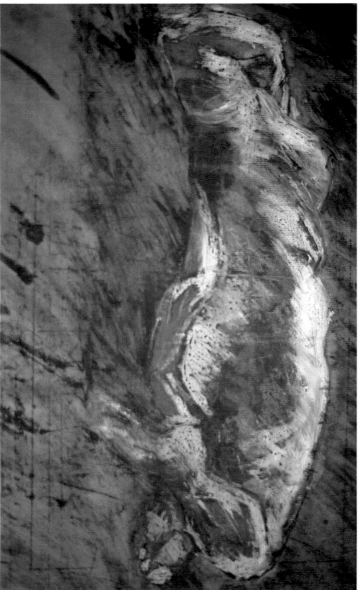

ABOVE
Viv Levy
Reclining Nude
Charcoal, removed and manipulated with bread. I started by dredging the page with charcoal and then found the patterns of light by removing the black pigment, and reapplying it when I was able to discern the semi-tones.

LEFT
Viv Levy
Reclining Nude
White oil crayon, black wash.
This was done the other way round. I found the light with white oil pastel on brown paper and then washed over it with a black ink wash.

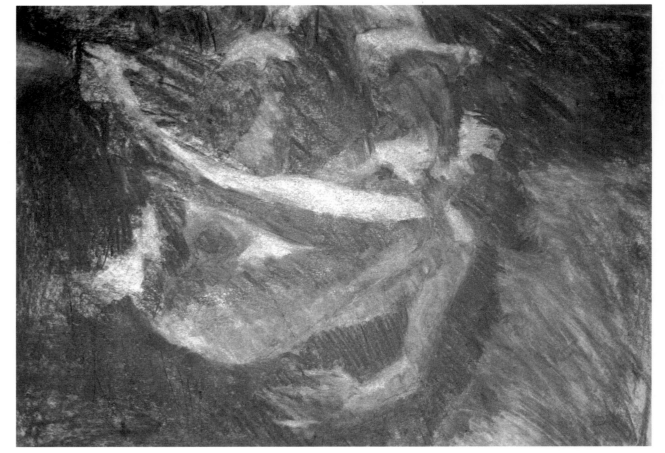